amos lee

CONTENTS

2 Keep It Loose, Keep It Tight

7 Seen It All Before

20 Arms of a Woman

31 Give It Up

35 Dreamin'

44 Soul Suckers

53 Colors

59 Bottom of the Barrel

67 Black River

75 Love in the Lies

84 All My Friends

88 *Guitar Notation Legend*

This book was approved by Amos Lee

Front cover photo by Clay Patrick McBride
Back cover photo by Denise Guerin

Transcribed by Paul Pappas

Cherry Lane Music Company
Director of Publications/Project Editor: Mark Phillips
Manager of Publications: Gabrielle Fastman

ISBN: 978-1-60378-027-8

Visit our website at www.cherrylane.com

KEEP IT LOOSE, KEEP IT TIGHT

Words and Music by
Amos Lee

oh, who we are ___ not. _____ I think we got ___ a

chance _____ to make it right. _____ But keep it loose,

keep it tight, _____ keep it

Verse
Gtr. 1: w/ Riff A

tight. _____ 3. I'm in love ___ with a girl ___ who's in love ___ with the world, ___ though I can't ___

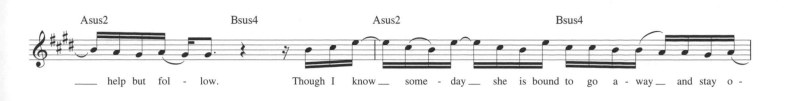

help but fol - low.   Though I know __ some - day __ she is bound to go a - way __ and stay o -

Gtr. 1: w/ Rhy. Fig. 2 (2 times)

- ver the rain - bow.   Got - ta learn __ how to let her __ go _____   o -

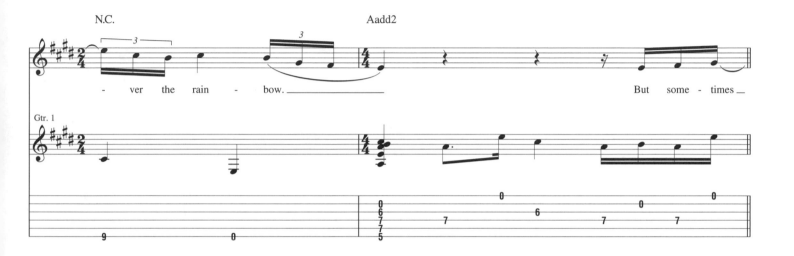

- ver the rain - bow. _____   But some - times __

Gtr. 1

Chorus

__ we for - get   who we got,   who they are, _____

oh,   who they   are __ not. _____   There is so __

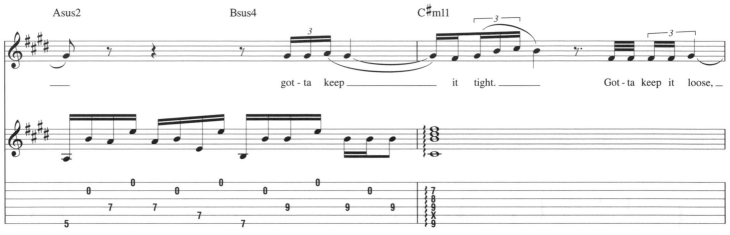

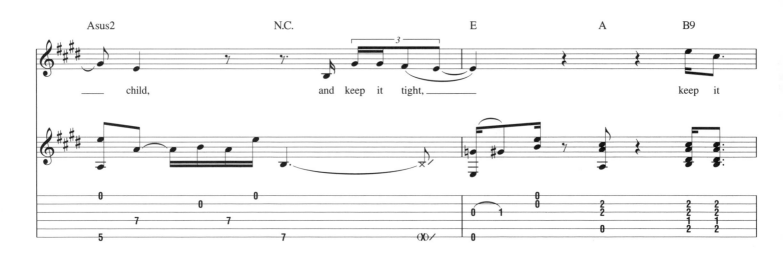

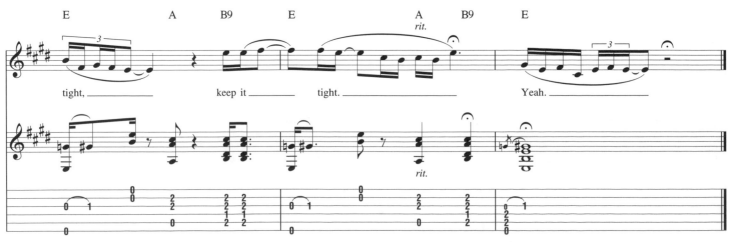

SEEN IT ALL BEFORE

Words and Music by
Amos Lee

1. Go a-head, ba-by, run a-way a-gain.

Grow-ing tired of chas-ing you.

7

I know you on - ly have time _____ to love _____ me. _____

You've got _____ noth - ing bet - ter to do.

Pre-Chorus

Who's bold e - nough to _____ be - lieve _____

8

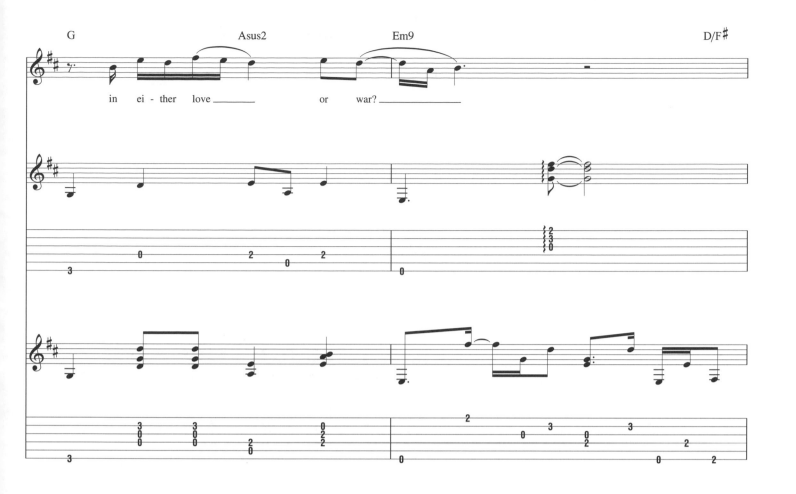

in ei - ther love _____ or war? _____

Both just leave you bust - ed   and bro - ken down _____   and want - ing more. __

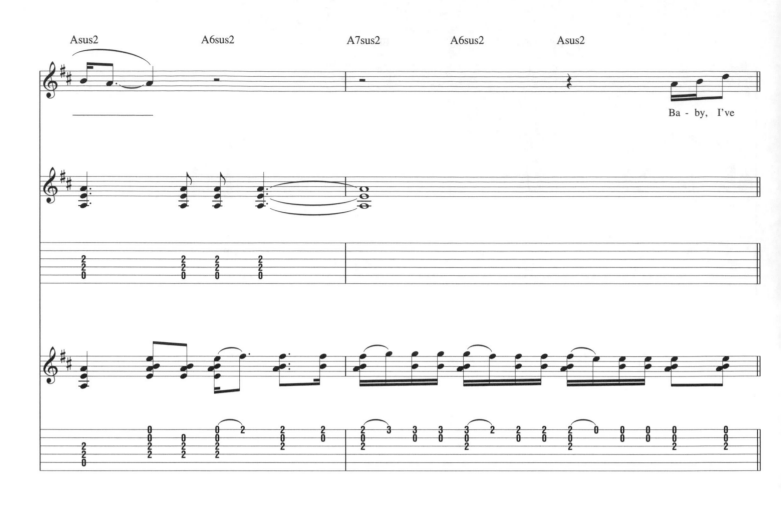

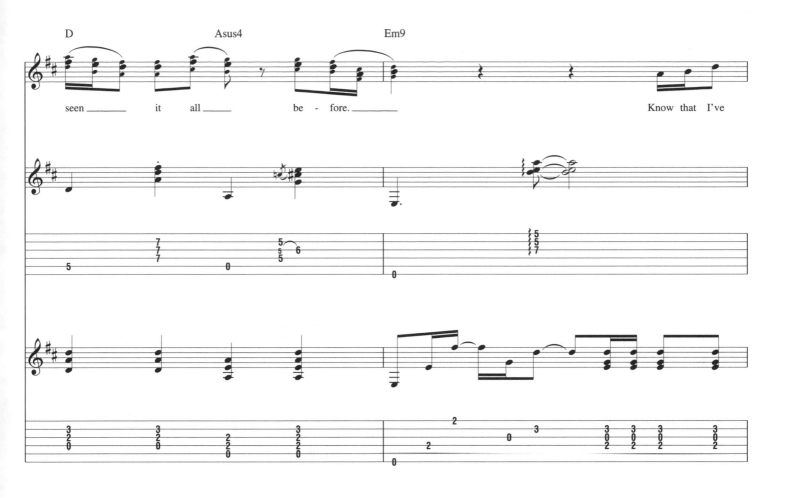

seen _____ it all _____ be - fore. _____   Know that I've

seen _____ it all _____ be - fore. _____   And I ain't gon - na

End Rhy. Fig. 1

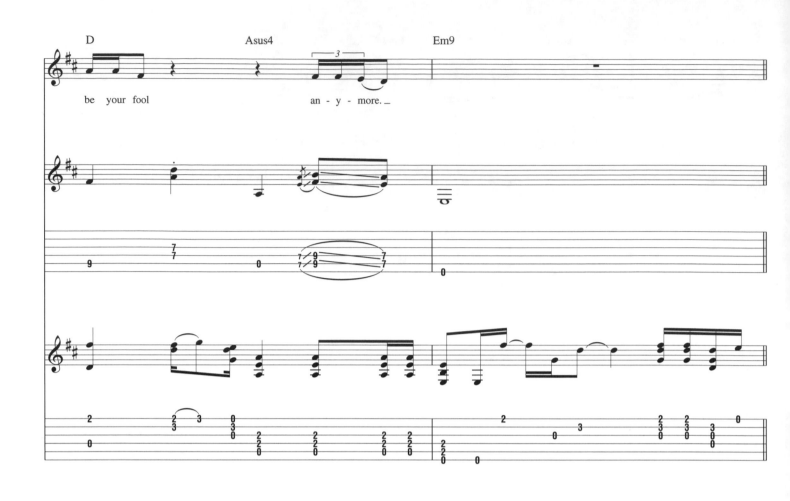

be   your fool   an - y - more. _

Verse

2. I can hear my heart _ pound - ing,

oh, _____ but I _____ just can't de - cide. _____

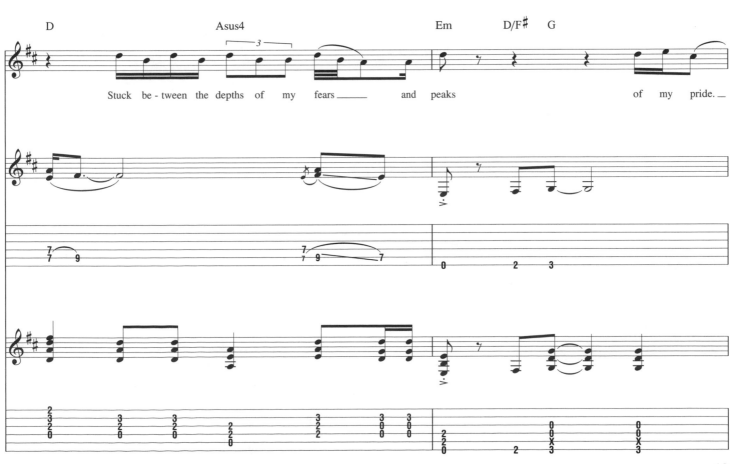

Stuck be - tween the depths of my fears _____ and peaks of my pride. __

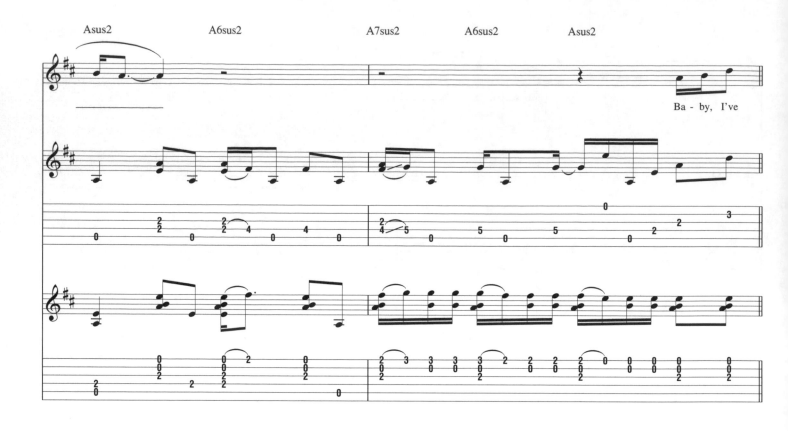

Chorus

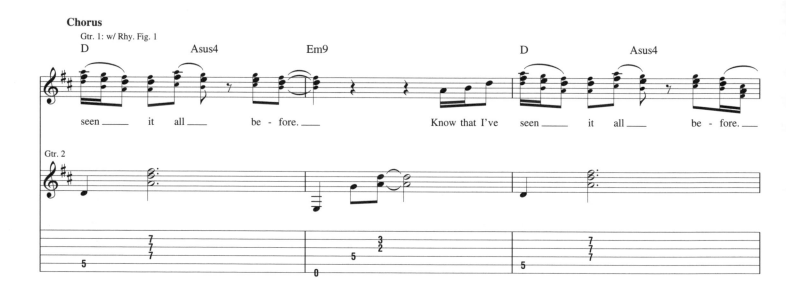

14

be your fool an-y-more. Yeah.

I've seen ev - 'ry - thing _____ your _____

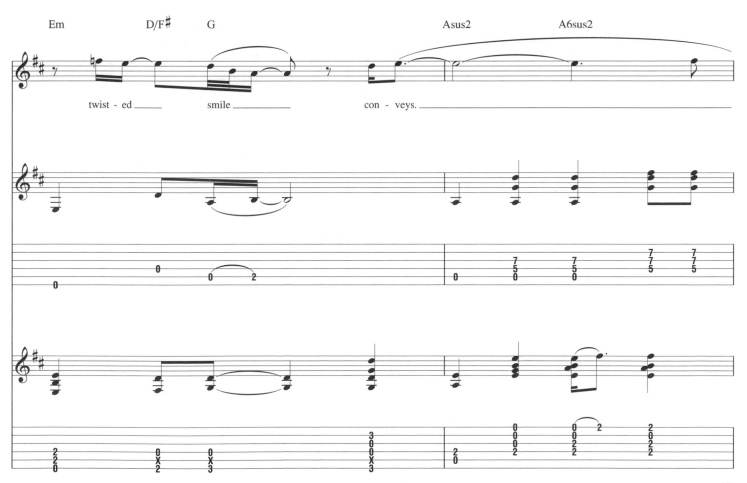

twist - ed _____ smile _____ con - veys. _____

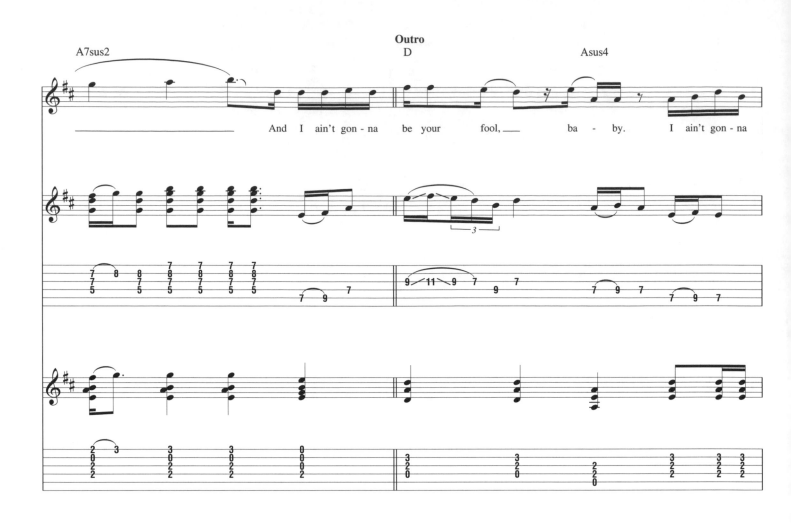

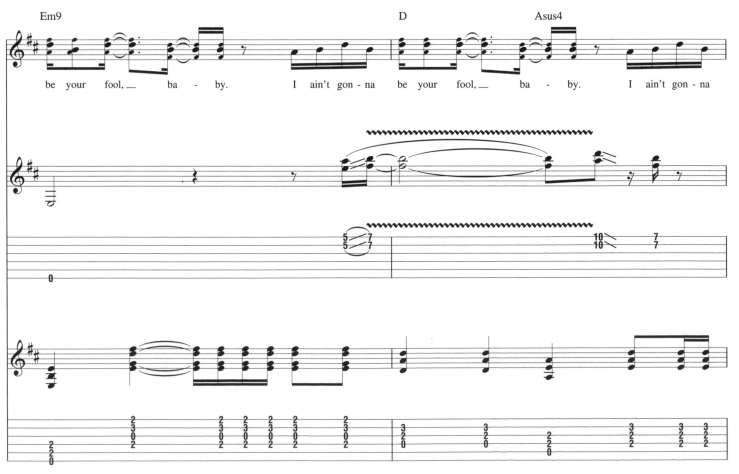

be your fool, __ ba - by. I ain't gon - na be your fool, __ ba - by. I ain't gon - na

be your fool, __ ba - by. I ain't gon - na be your fool, __ ba - by, an - y - more. __

ARMS OF A WOMAN

Words and Music by
Amos Lee

lone.

A thou-sand miles __

_____ from the place I was born, but when she

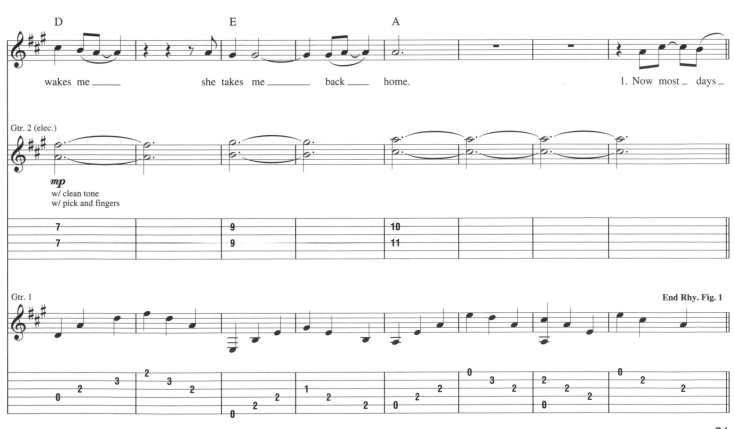

wakes me _____ she takes me _____ back _____ home.

1. Now most _ days _

Verse

Gtr. 1: w/ Rhy. Fig. 1 (1st 20 meas.)

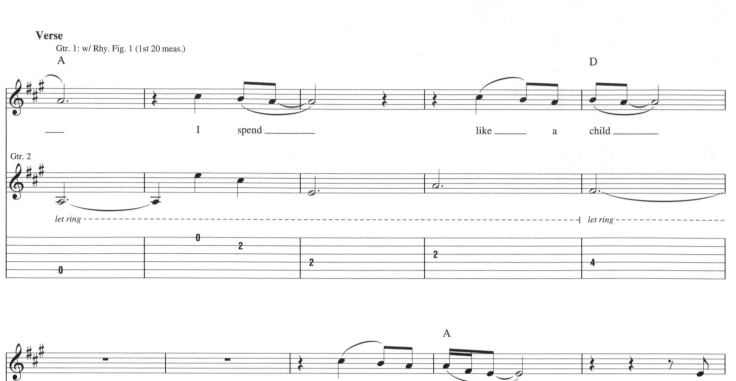

I spend _____ like _____ a child _____

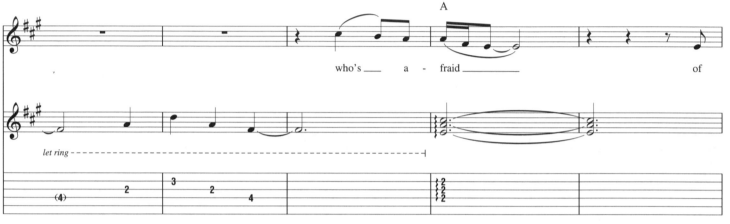

who's _____ a - fraid _____ of

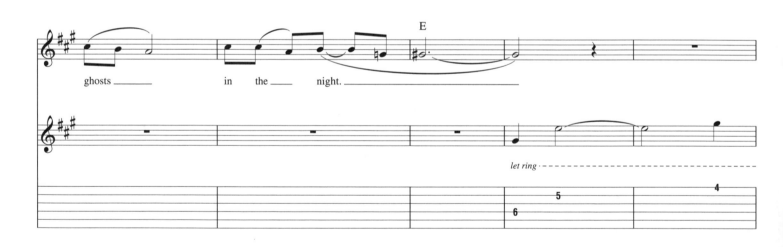

ghosts _____ in the _____ night. _____

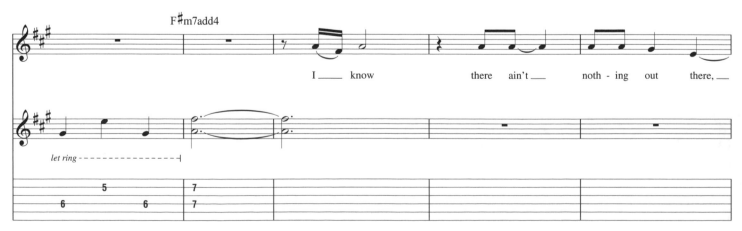

I _____ know there ain't _____ noth - ing out there, _____

Chorus
Gtr. 1: w/ Rhy. Fig. 1

23

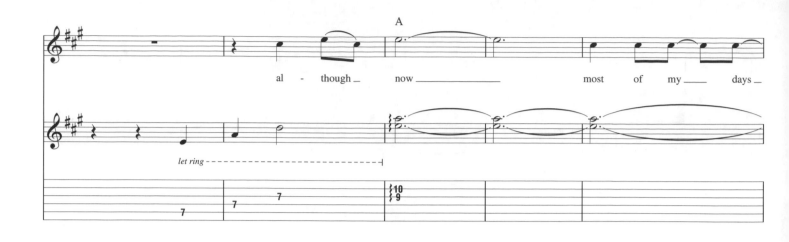

al - though _ now _ most of my _ days _

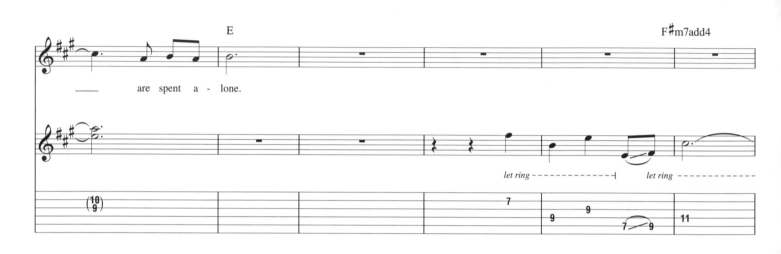

_ are spent a - lone.

F#m7add4

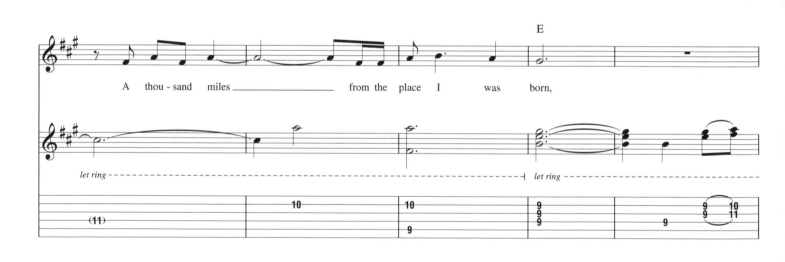

A thou - sand miles _ from the place I was born,

but when she wakes me _ she takes me _

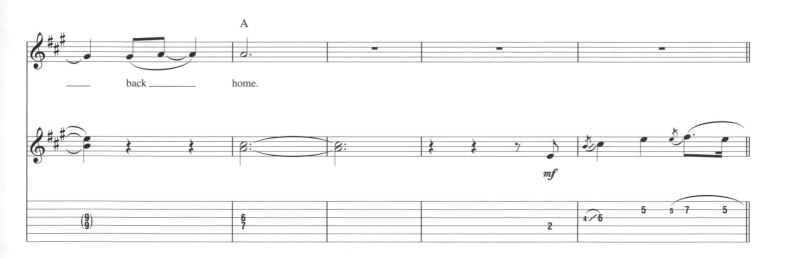

back _____ home.

Guitar Solo

let ring -

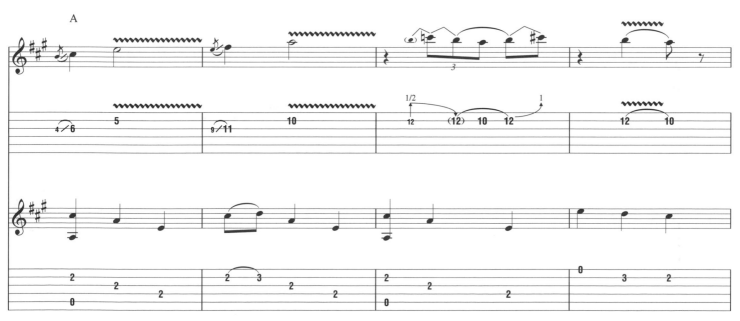

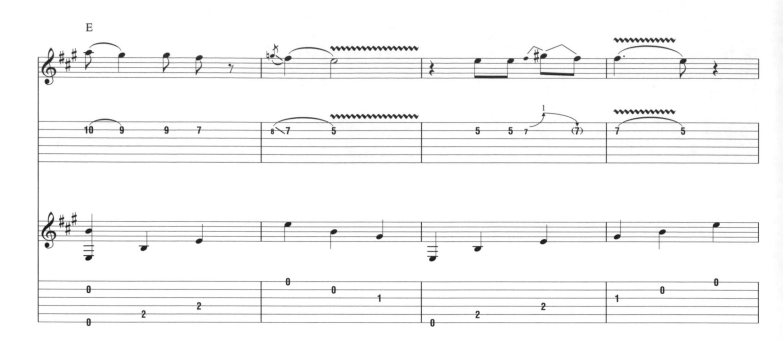

Chorus
Gtr. 1: w/ Rhy. Fig. 1 (last 16 meas.)

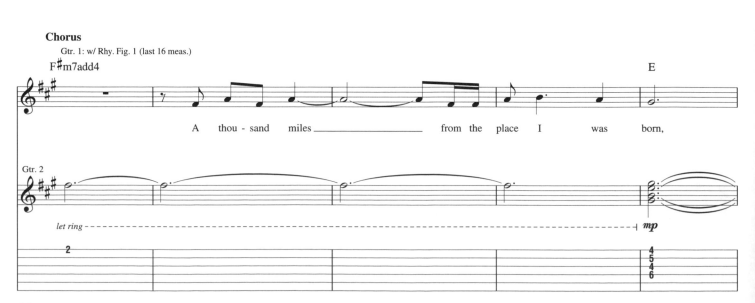

A thou-sand miles _____ from the place I was born,

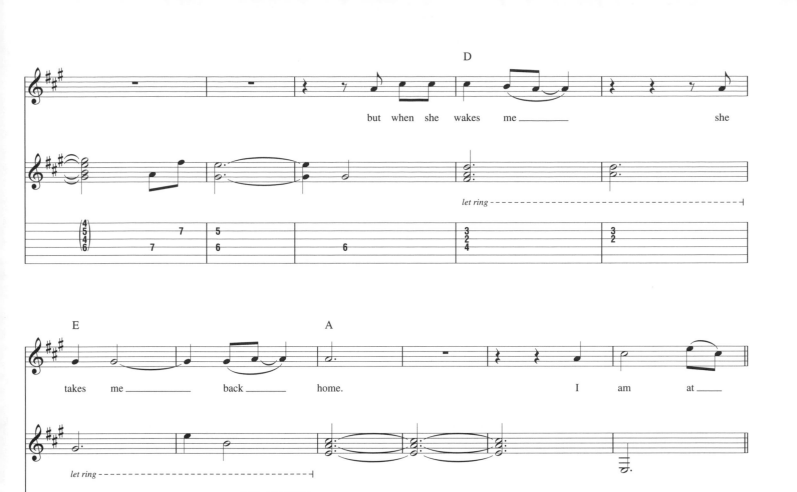

but when she wakes me _____ she

takes me _____ back _____ home. I am at _____

Outro-Chorus
Gtr. 1: w/ Rhy. Fig. 1 (1st 24 meas.)

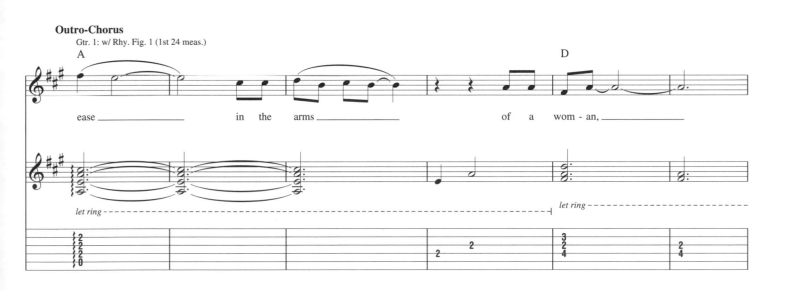

ease _____ in the arms _____ of a wom-an, _____

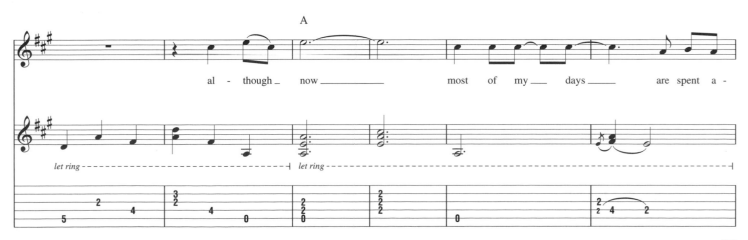

al - though __ now _____ most of my __ days _____ are spent a-

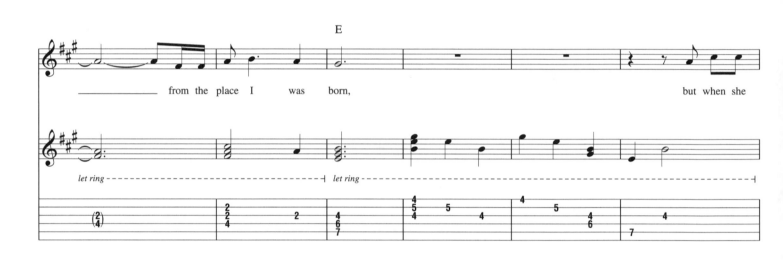

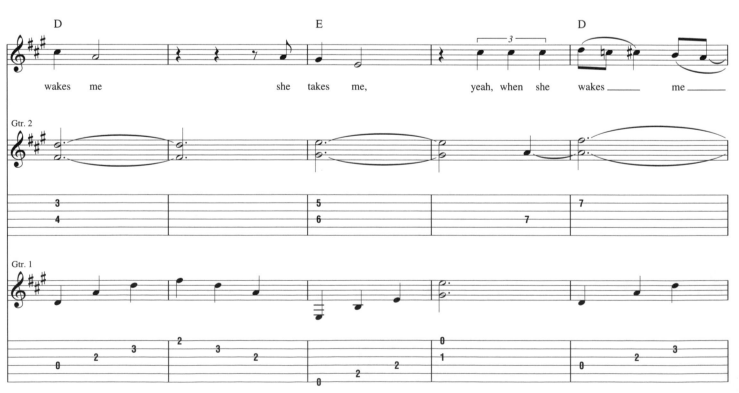

28

she takes me, yeah, when she wakes ___ me ___ she

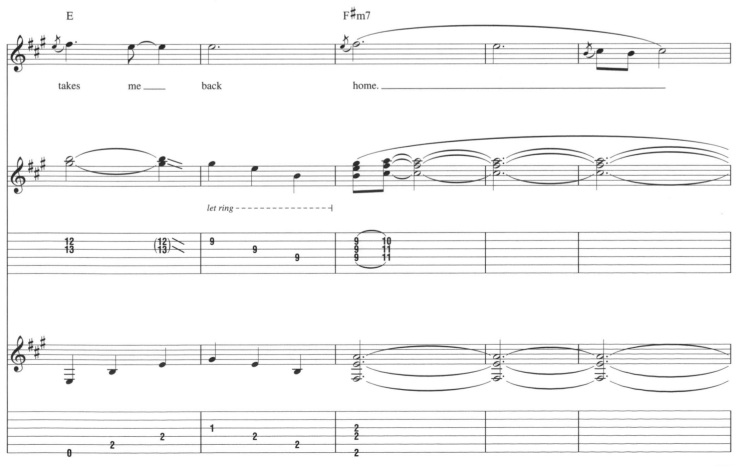

takes me ___ back home. ___

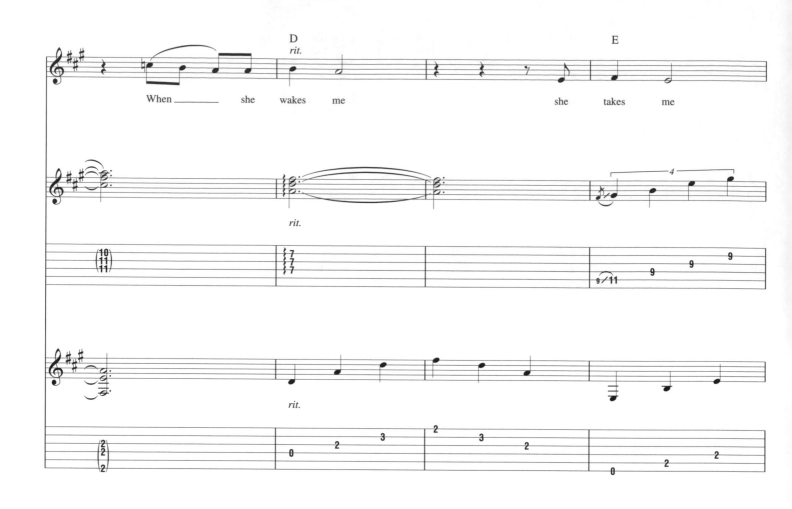

When _____ she wakes me she takes me

back _____ home. _____

GIVE IT UP

Words and Music by
Amos Lee

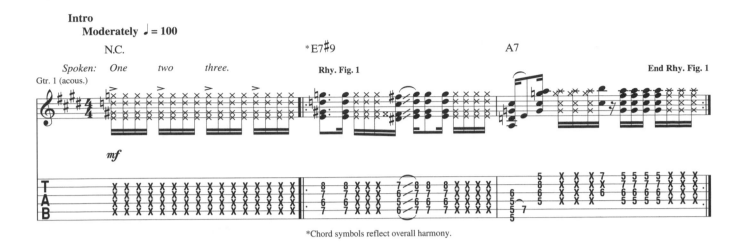

*Chord symbols reflect overall harmony.

Verse

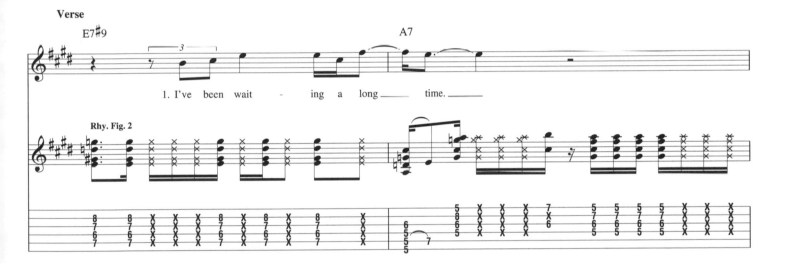

1. I've been wait - ing a long time.

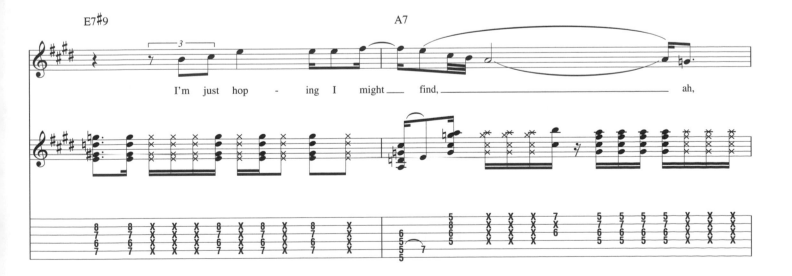

I'm just hop - ing I might find, ah,

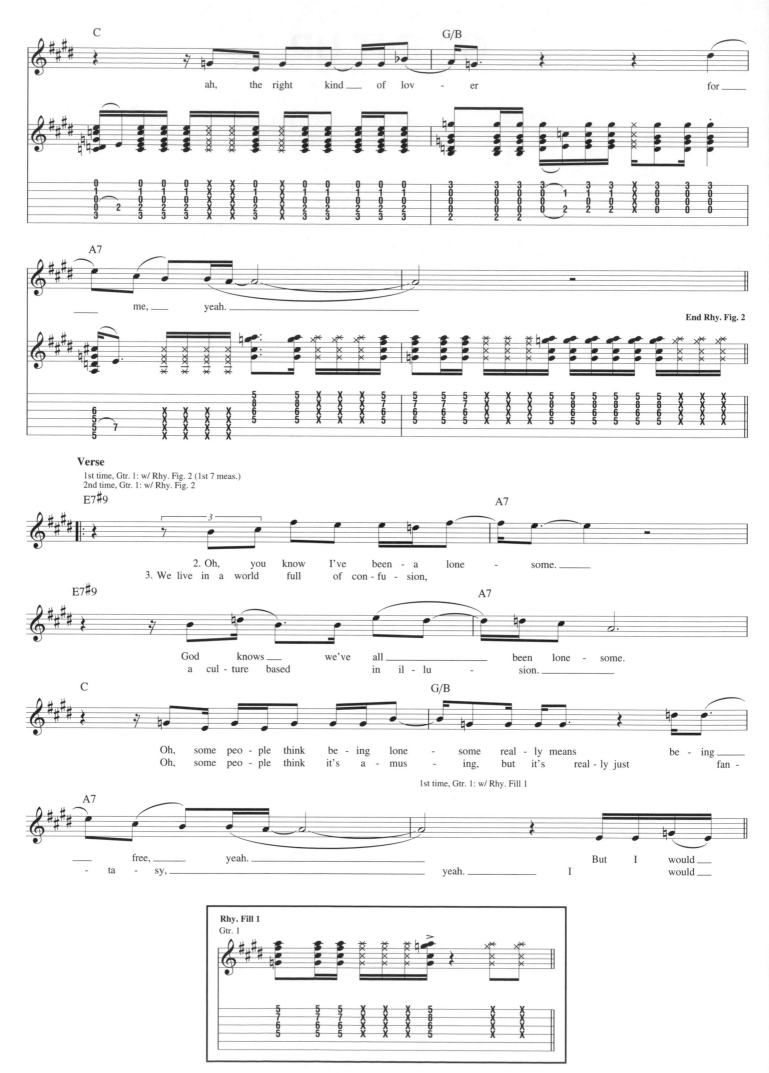

DREAMIN'

Words and Music by
Amos Lee

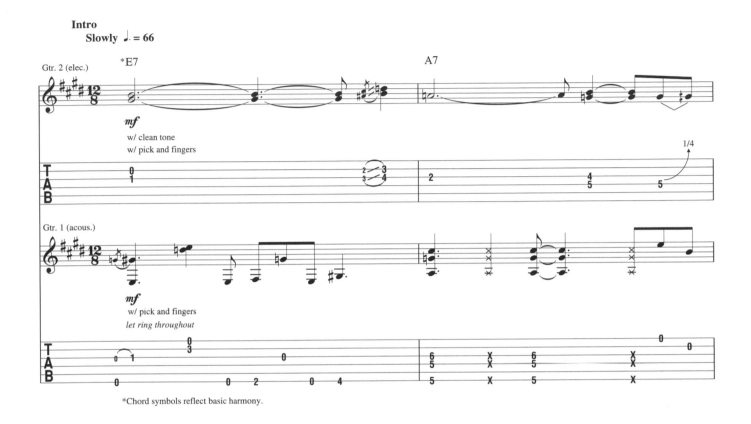

*Chord symbols reflect basic harmony.

is as o - pen as _____ the sky. _____

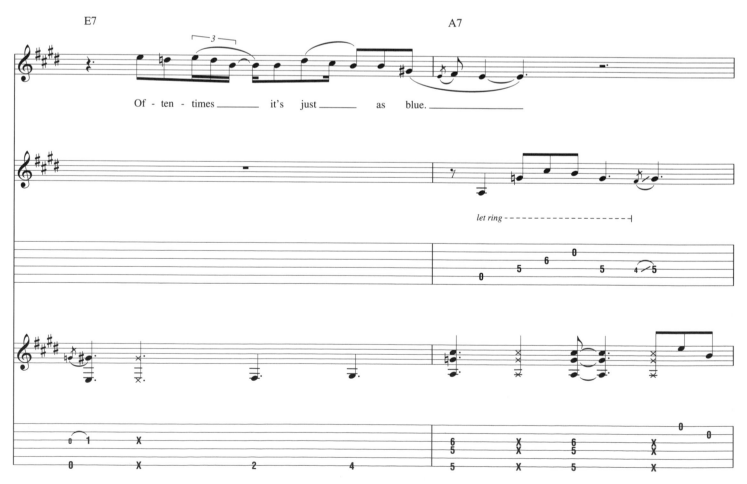

Of - ten - times _____ it's just _____ as blue. _____

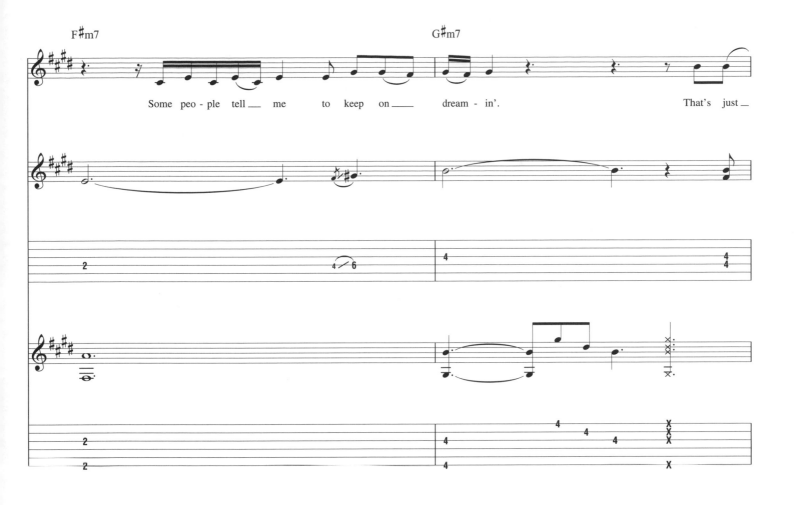

Some peo - ple tell ___ me to keep on ___ dream - in'. That's just ___

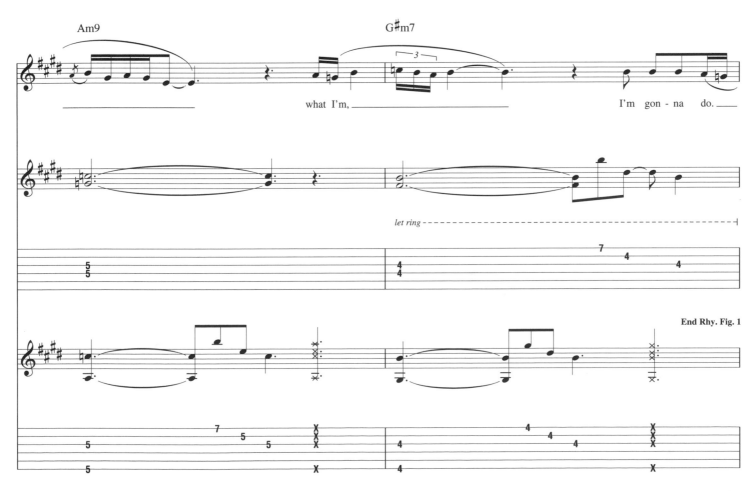

___ what I'm, ___ I'm gon - na do. ___

let ring -

End Rhy. Fig. 1

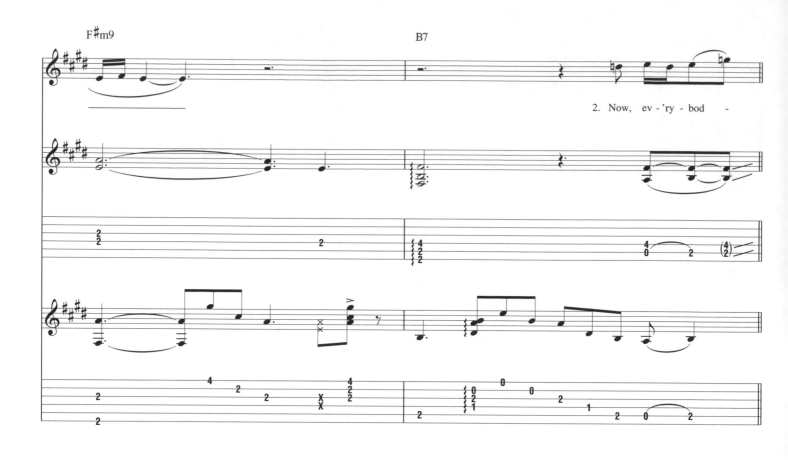

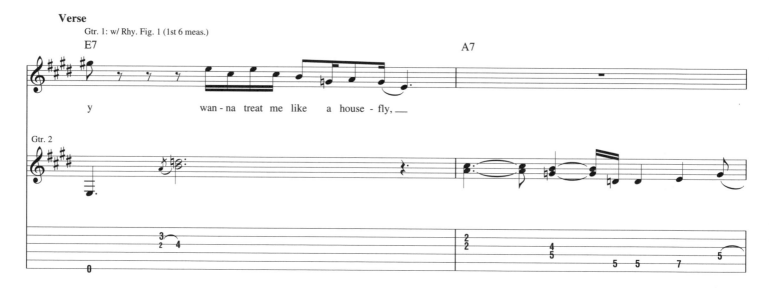

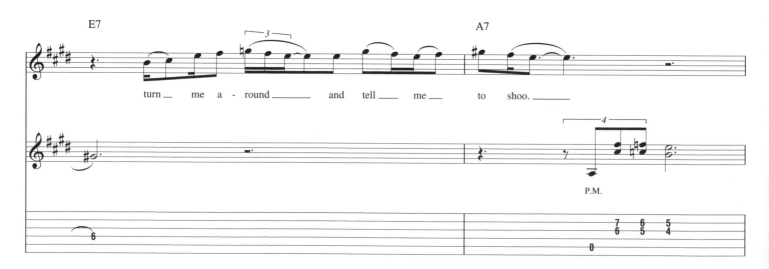

Bridge

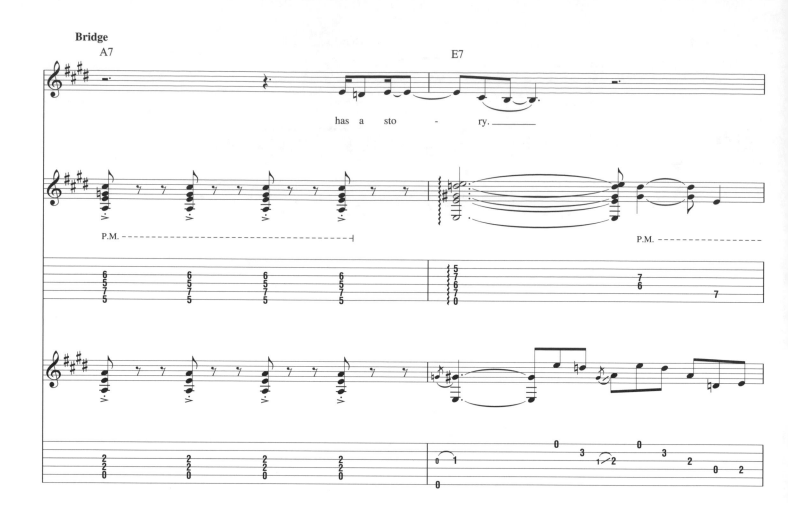

has a sto - ry.

Ev - 'ry hand ____ needs _____ a glove. ____

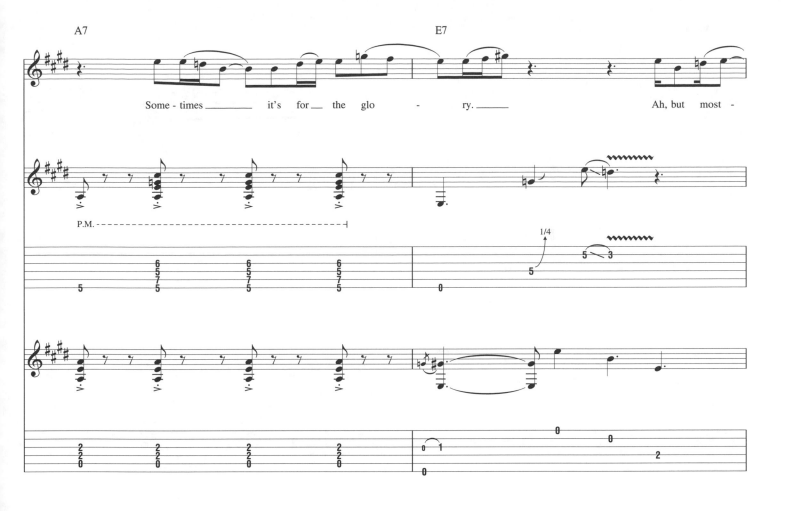

Some - times _____ it's for _ the glo - ry. _____   Ah, but most -

- ly _____   it's for the love. _____   3. It's the love, _____

that's _____ just what I'm ___ gon - na do. __

Mm. _____

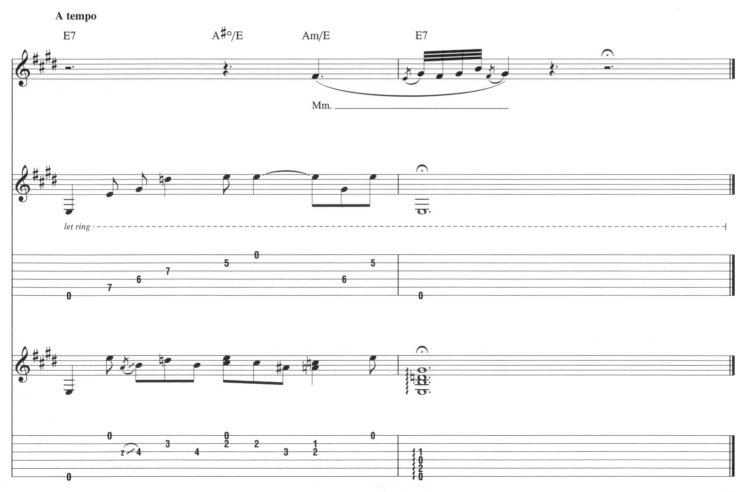

SOUL SUCKERS

Words and Music by
Amos Lee

Gtr. 2: Drop D tuning:
(low to high) D-A-D-G-B-E

Intro
Moderately slow ♩ = 74

*Gtr. 2

*Strings arr. for gtr.

mp
w/ fingers

Gtr. 1 (acous.)

mp
w/ pick and fingers
let ring throughout

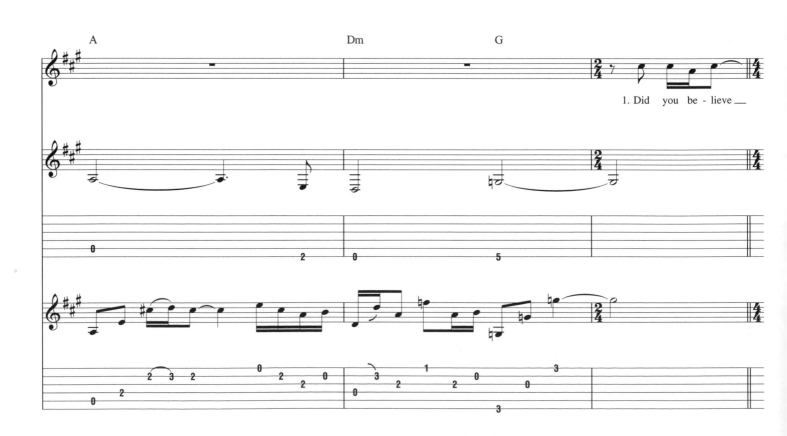

1. Did you be - lieve ___

46

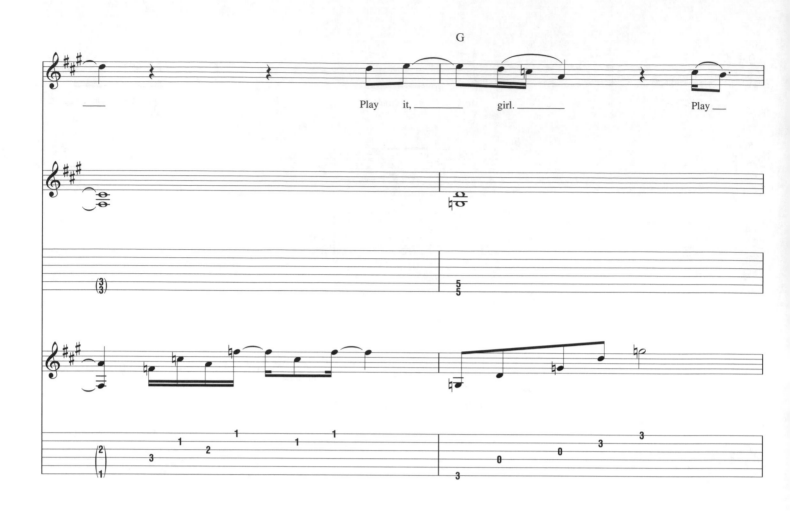

Play it, _____ girl. _____ Play _____

it, girl. _____ Play _____ it, girl. _____

48

Verse

Gtr. 1: w/ Riff A (1st 6 meas.)
Gtr. 2 tacet

Gtr. 2

3. Does it make you feel ____ good ____ when they tell ____ you what ____ you ____ want ____ to hear? ____ And af - ter they ____ suck all your soul, ____ well, ____ that's when ____ they'll dis - ap - pear. ____ They'll dis - ap -

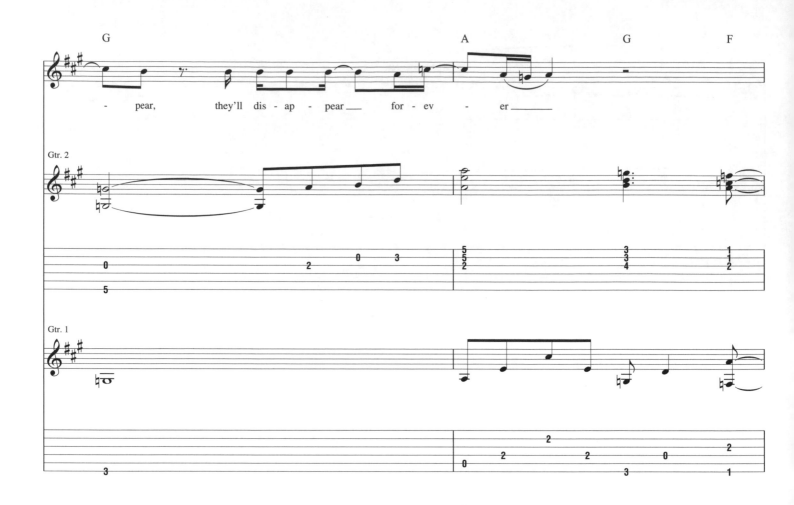

- pear,   they'll dis - ap - pear___ for - ev - er___

like___ a prince___   in your lit - tle___ fair - y___

tale. ___ And you ___ will find ___ the day ___

___ when ___ they put your ___ soul ___ on ___ sale. ___

Noth - ing could be fur - ther from the truth, __ my love. __ And

noth - ing is more pow - er - ful than beau - ty in a wick - ed world. __

COLORS

Words and Music by
Amos Lee

Intro
Slowly ♩ = 64

*Chord symbols reflect implied harmony.

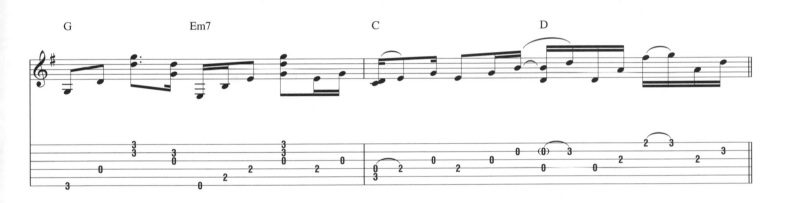

Verse

1. Yes - ter - day ___ I got lost ___ in ___ the cir - cus,

feel - in' like ___ such ___ a ___ mess. ___

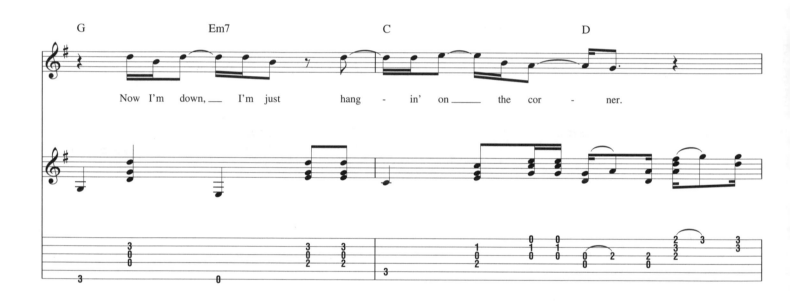

Now I'm down, ___ I'm just hang - in' on ___ the cor - ner.

I can't help but ___ rem - i - nisce. ___ 'Cause when ___ you're

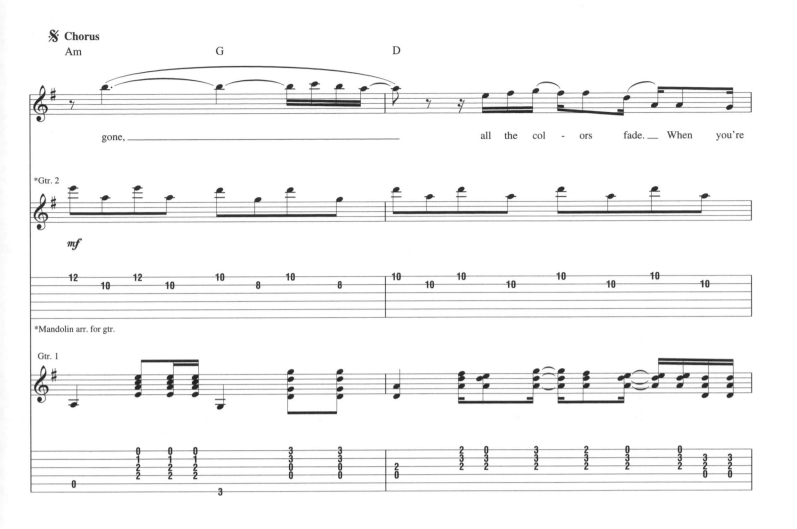

gone, _____ all the col - ors fade. __ When you're

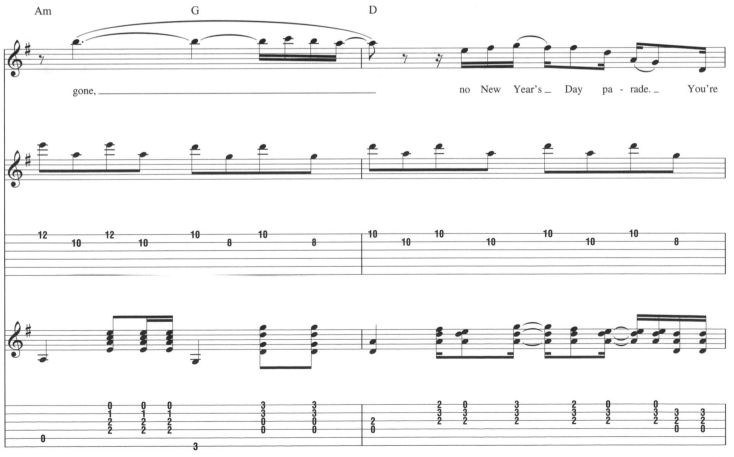

gone, _____ no New Year's __ Day pa - rade. __ You're

gone; _____ col - ors seem _ to fade. _

Verse

2. Your ma - ma called; _ she said that _____ you're down - stairs cry - in',

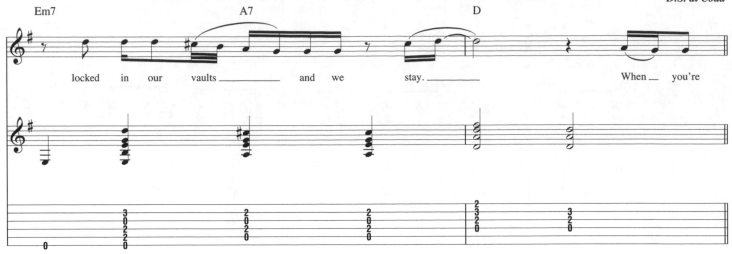

locked in our vaults _____ and we stay. _____ When _ you're

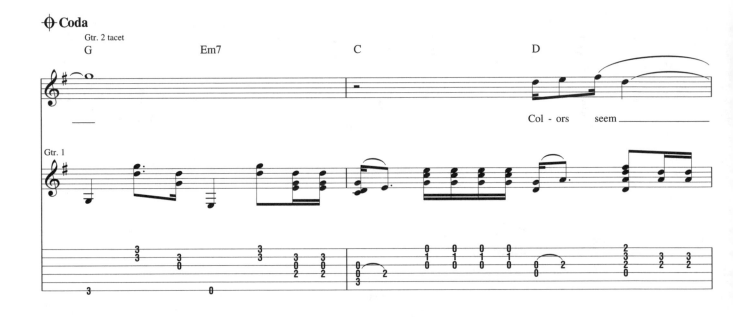

Col - ors seem _____

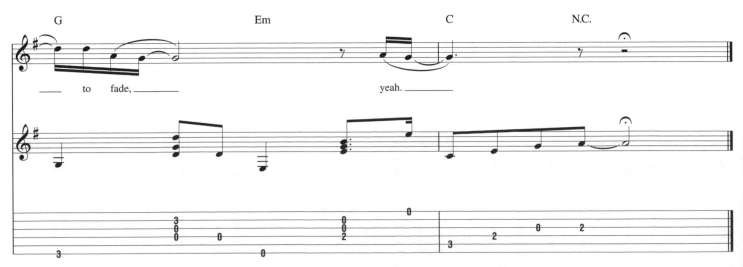

_ to fade, _____ yeah. _____

BOTTOM OF THE BARREL

Words and Music by
Amos Lee

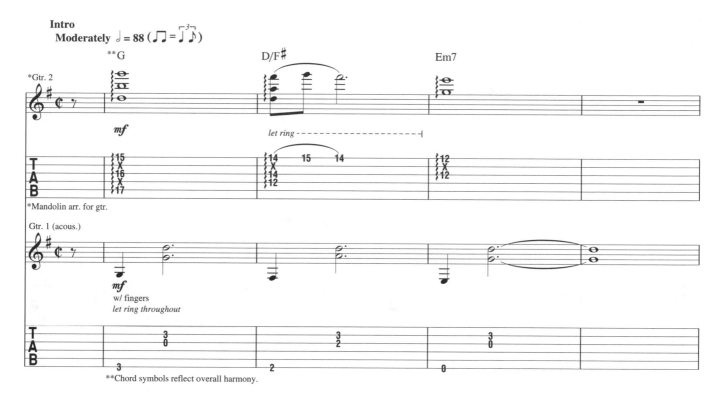

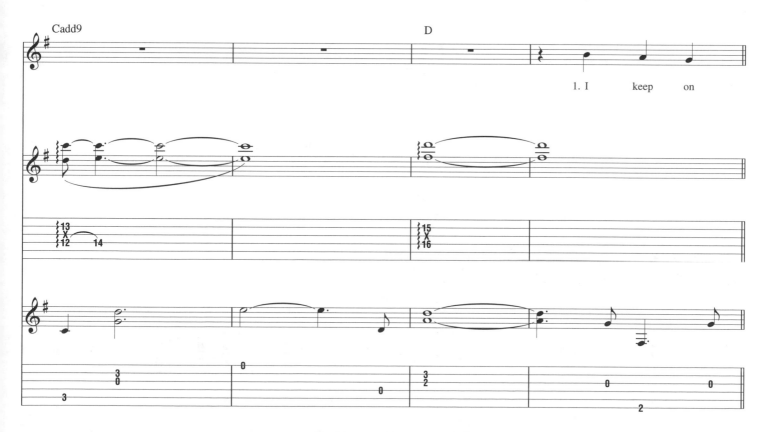

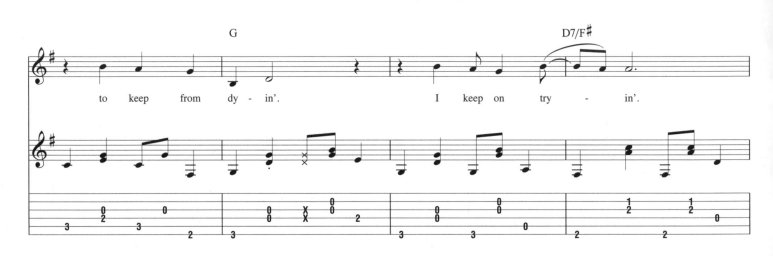

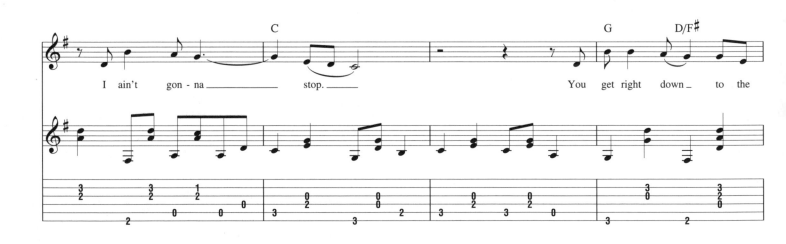

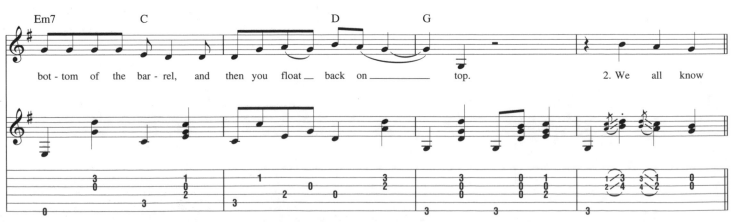

is al - ways __ green - er in some-

- one __ else - 's yard. __ And __ the world __

gets so ___ much   mean   -   er   when your heart ___

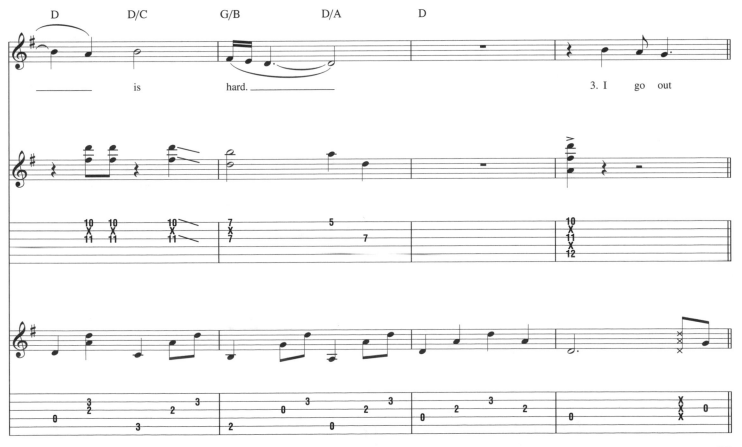

_____ is   hard. _____   3. I   go out

walk - in'   in   an - y   sea - son.   It   could   be

rain - in',   it   could   be   freez - in'.   I   don't   need   no   rea-

son; it's just so pleas - in' I ___ can't _____ stop. _____ You

get right down _ to the bot - tom of the bar - rel, and then you float _ back on _____ top. You

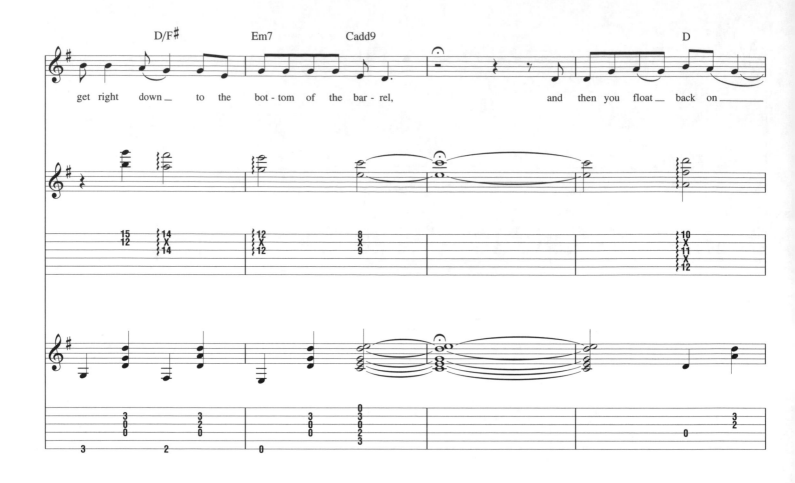

get right down ___ to the bot-tom of the bar-rel, and then you float ___ back on ___

___ top. Oh, ___ yeah. Oh, ___ ba - by, come on.

BLACK RIVER

Words and Music by
Amos Lee

Gtr. 1 tuning:
(low to high) D-A-D-F♯-B-E
Gtr. 2: Open D tuning:
(low to high) D-A-D-F♯-A-D

Intro
Moderately slow ♩ = 72

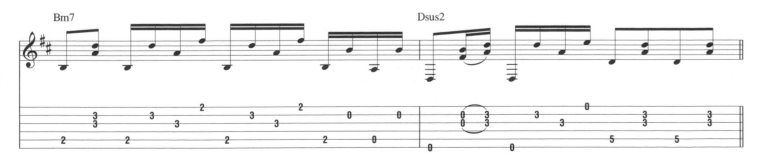

67

Verse

1. Woh, _____ black ___ riv - er _____

gon - na take my cares a - way. _____

Woh, _____ black ___ riv - er _____

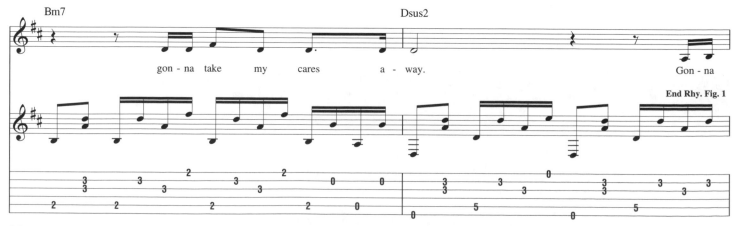

gon - na take my cares a - way. Gon - na

End Rhy. Fig. 1

take-a my cares, gon - na car - ry my cares, gon - na take-a my cares a - way. Gon - na

take-a my cares, gon - na car - ry my cares, gon - na take-a my cares __ a - way.

Verse

Gtr. 1: w/ Rhy. Fig. 1

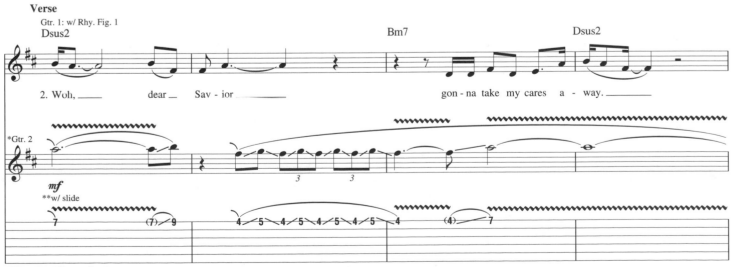

2. Woh, ____ dear __ Sav - ior ____ gon - na take my cares a - way. ____ Woh,

*Gtr. 2

**w/ slide

*Resonator guitar arr. for gtr.

**Notes are not struck; vibrato and slide movement cause notes to sound (next 8 meas.).

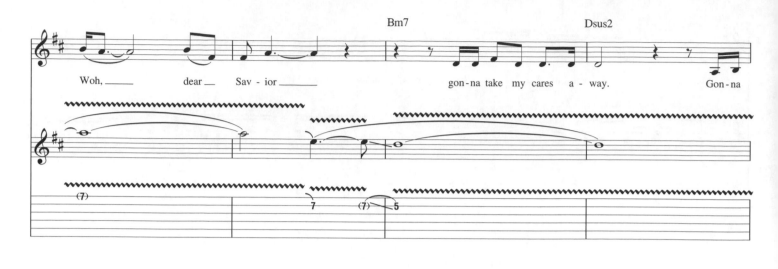

Woh, ____ dear ___ Sav - ior _____ gon - na take my cares a - way. Gon - na

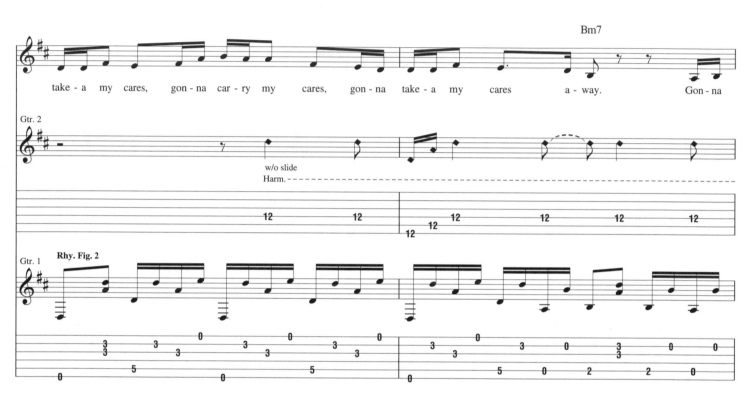

take - a my cares, gon - na car - ry my cares, gon - na take - a my cares a - way. Gon - na

take - a my cares, gon - na car - ry my cares, gon - na take - a my cares _ a - way.

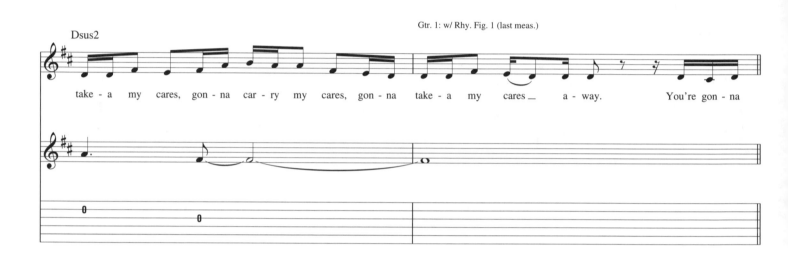

Bridge

72

take all of the sad - ness in - side _ of me. _ Gon-na take it all _ and set _ me free. _

let ring

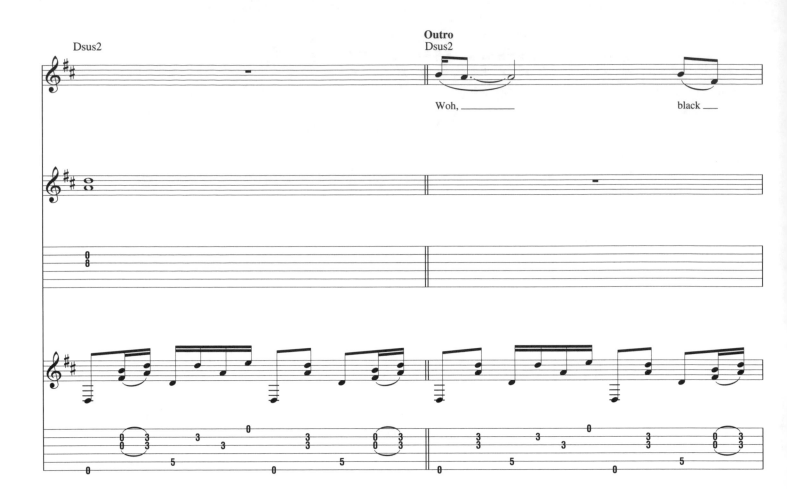

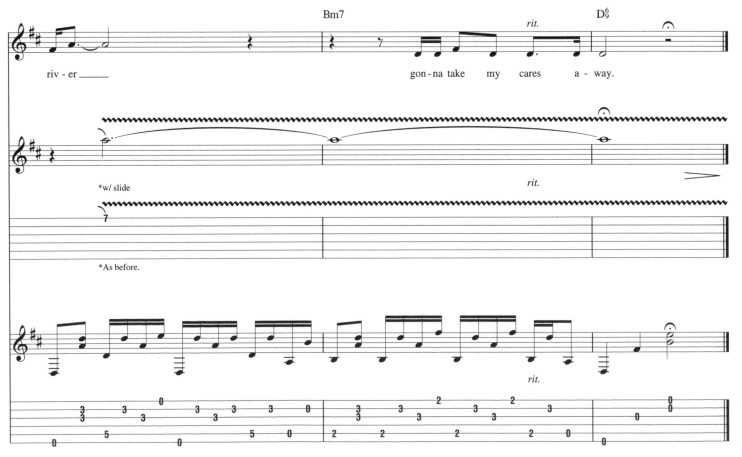

LOVE IN THE LIES

Words and Music by
Amos Lee

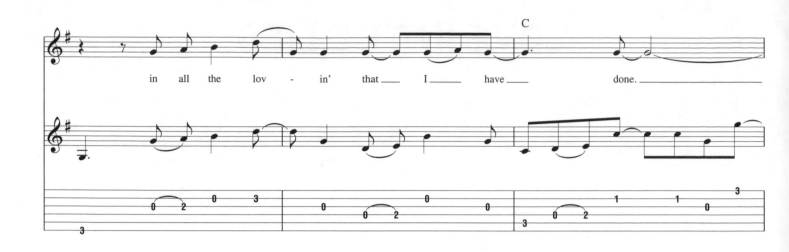

in all the lov - in' that ___ I ___ have ___ done. _____

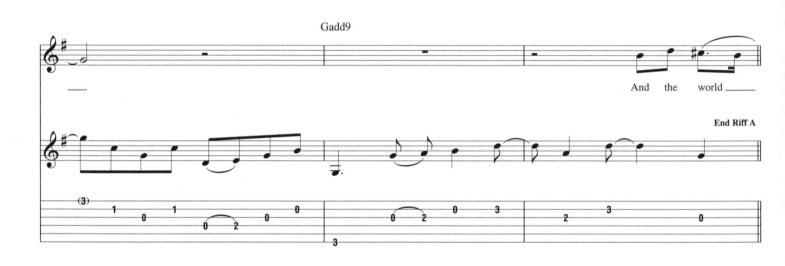

___ And the world _____

And the world _____

Chorus

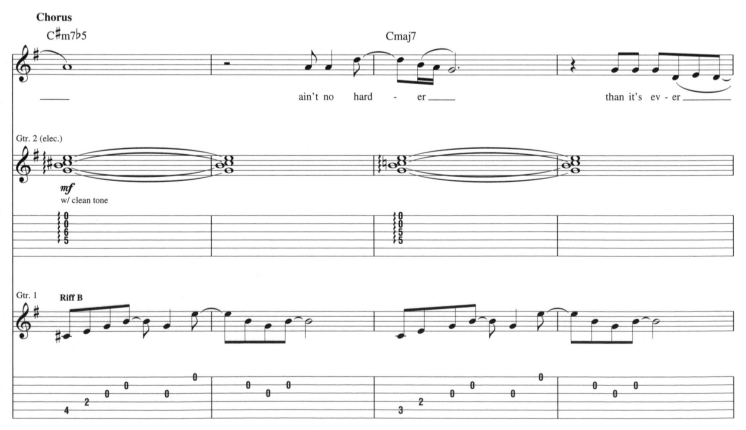

_____ ain't no hard - er _____ than it's ev - er _____

Gtr. 2 (elec.)

mf
w/ clean tone

Gtr. 1 Riff B

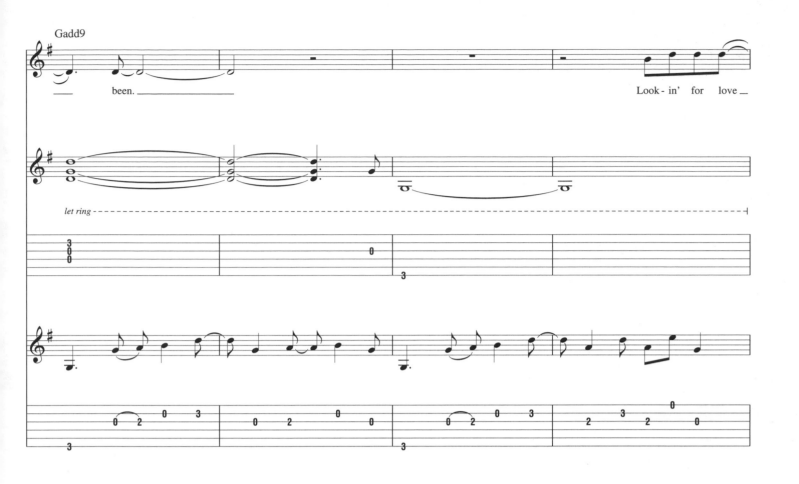

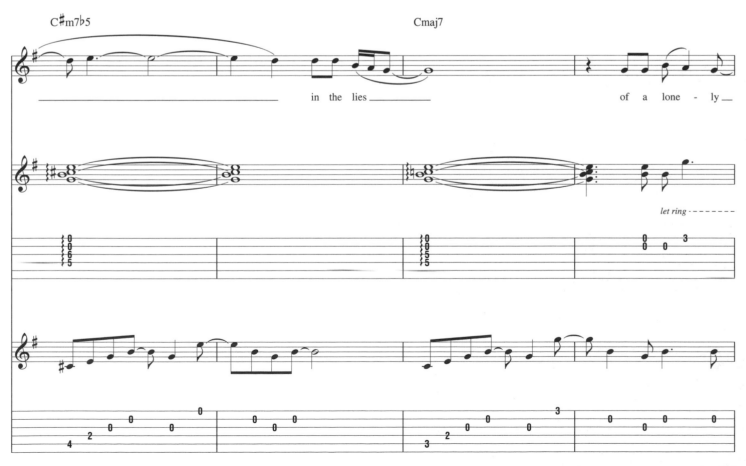

friend.

Verse
Gtr. 1: w/ Riff A
Gtr. 2 tacet

Gadd9

2. And so much su - per - sti - tion, ___ and so much wor - ry in ___ my ___

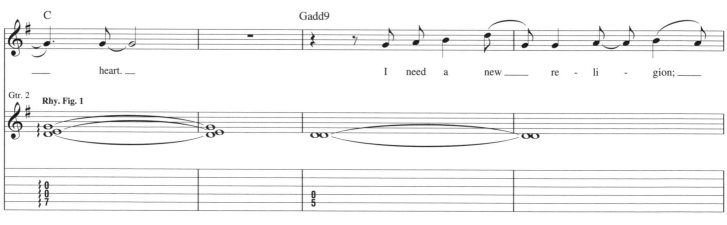

___ heart. ___

I need a new ___ re - li - gion; ___

Gtr. 2 Rhy. Fig. 1

it's time to make ___ a brand - new ___ start. ___

End Rhy. Fig. 1

Now we're back _____ in New _ York _ Cit - y   look - in' for love _

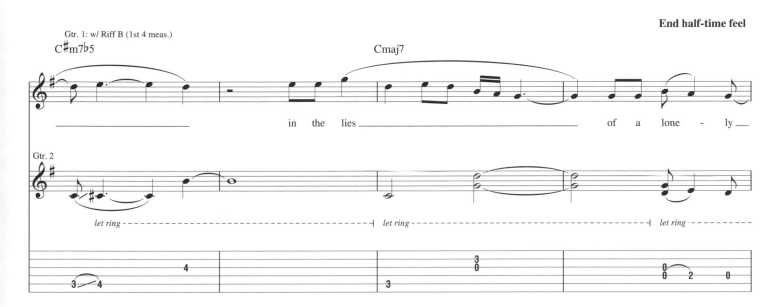

Gtr. 1: w/ Riff B (1st 4 meas.)

End half-time feel

_____ in the lies _____ of a lone - ly _

Gtr. 2

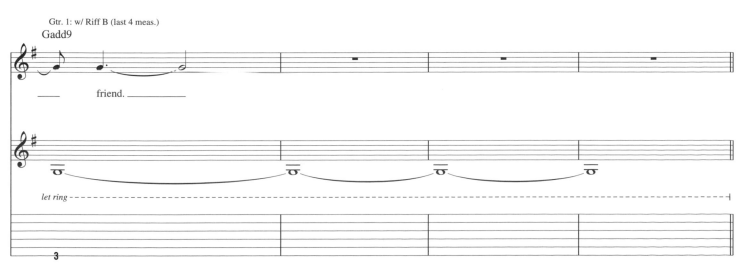

Gtr. 1: w/ Riff B (last 4 meas.)

_ friend. _

Verse

Gtr. 1: w/ Riff A
Gtr. 2 tacet

Gadd9

3. And now the clocks __ are run - ning, __ but no one knows __ where time __ goes. __

Gtr. 2: w/ Rhy. Fig. 1

C   Gadd9

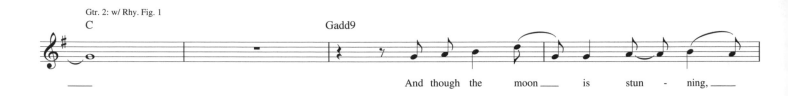

__ And though the moon __ is stun - ning, __

C

it's on - ly shad - ows that __ she __ shows. __

Chorus

Gtr. 1: w/ Riff B

Gadd9   C#m7♭5

Gtr. 2

And the world __ ain't no hard -

let ring -

Cmaj7   Gadd9

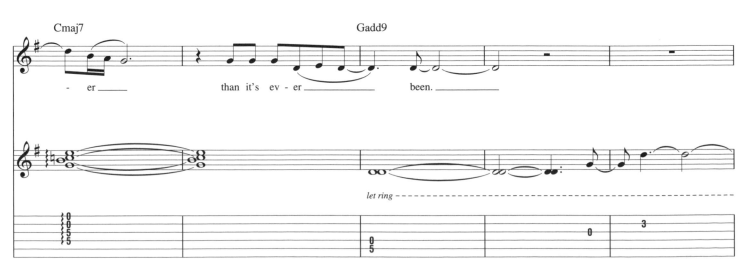

- er __ than it's ev - er __ been. __

let ring - - - - - - - - - - - - - - - - - -

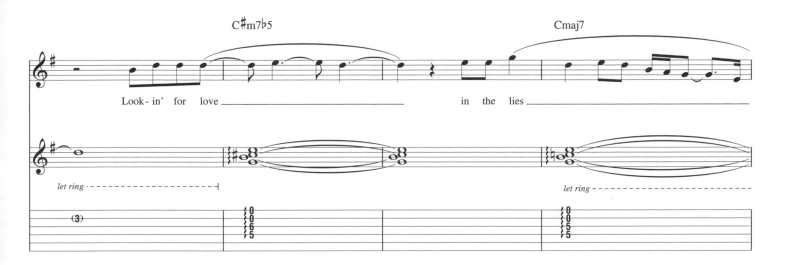

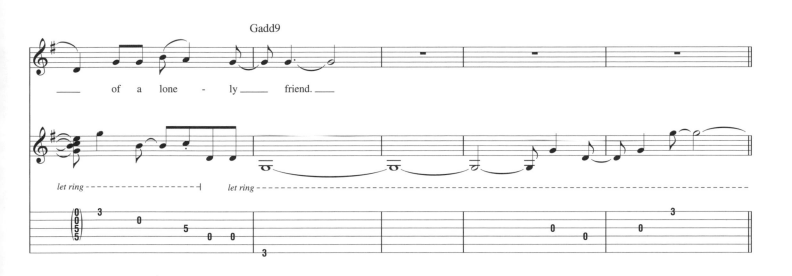

Outro

ALL MY FRIENDS

Words and Music by
Amos Lee

Drop D tuning:
(low to high) D-A-D-G-B-E

Intro
Slowly ♩ = 54

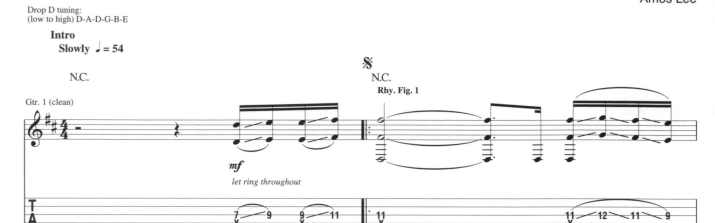

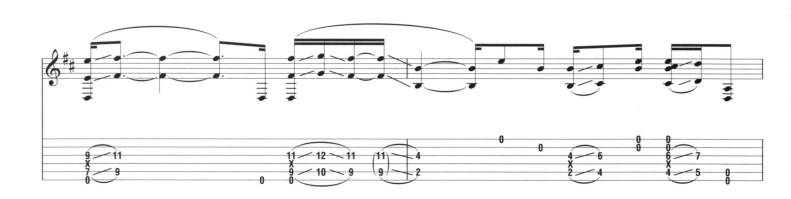

Verse

Gtr. 1: w/ Rhy. Fig. 1 (1 3/4 times)

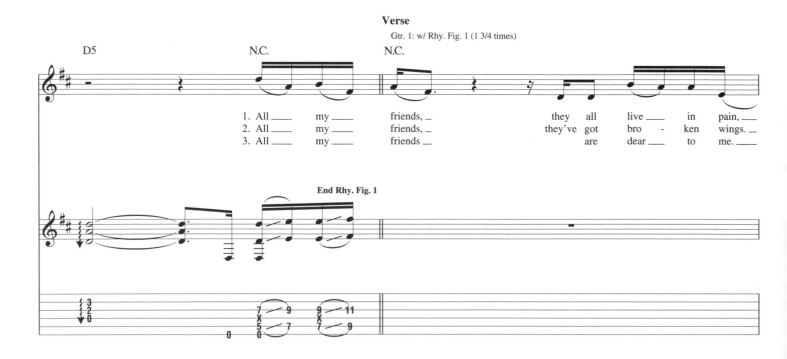

1. All ____ my ____ friends, ____ they all live ____ in pain, ____
2. All ____ my ____ friends, ____ they've got bro-ken wings. ____
3. All ____ my ____ friends ____ are dear ____ to me. ____

long - ing for the warmth _ of child - hood _ to bring 'em home _ a - gain. _
Nev - er will you hear _ them ask - ing why _ the caged _ bird
Oh, when the storm _ comes, _ they're as close _ as fam - i - ly. _

D5 N.C.

_ sings.
_ All _ my _ friends, _ they've got bro - ken hearts. _
All _ my _ friends, _ they know how _ to live. _
All _ my _ friends _ are the ones _ I choose. _

And if the world's _ a stage, _ we're _ search - in' for our parts. _
Oh, so much sor - row _ and so _ much love _ to give. _
Oh, if I hear _ them knock - in', you know _ I can't _ re - fuse. _

Chorus

D Gadd9

We'll face the winds _____ that break the

Gtr. 1

To Coda ⊕

G/F♯ Em(add9)

strong - est of trees _ and beck - on for the sweet, soft _____ sum -

85

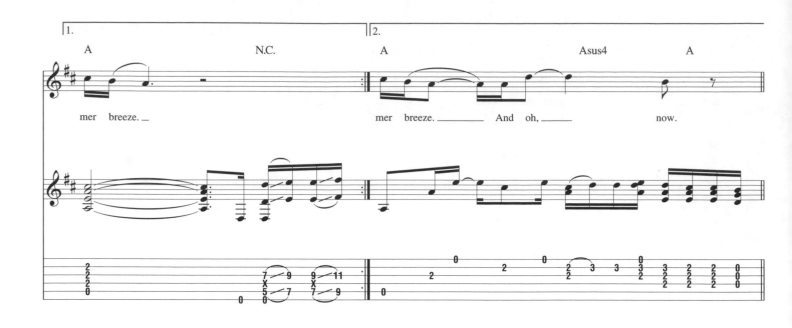

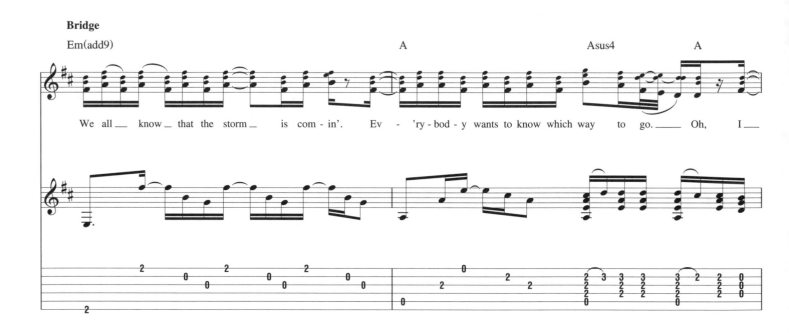

⊕ Coda

and beck-on for the sweet,___ soft___ sum-mer breeze.___ All___ my___

Outro

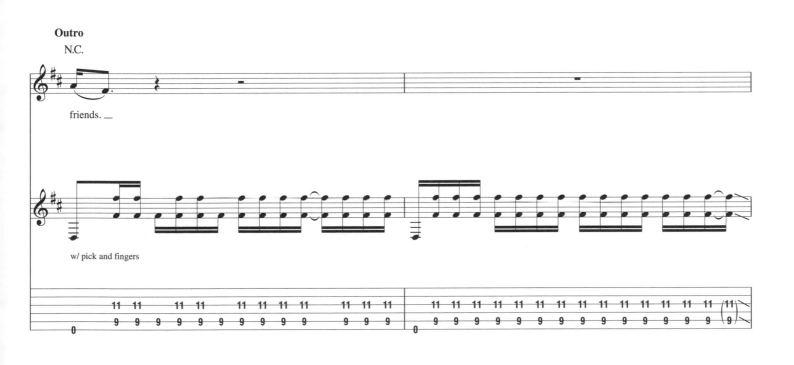

friends. _

w/ pick and fingers

Guitar Notation Legend

Guitar music can be notated three different ways: on a *musical staff*, in *tablature*, and in *rhythm slashes*.

RHYTHM SLASHES are written above the staff. Strum chords in the rhythm indicated. Use the chord diagrams found at the top of the first page of the transcription for the appropriate chord voicings. Round noteheads indicate single notes.

THE MUSICAL STAFF shows pitches and rhythms and is divided by bar lines into measures. Pitches are named after the first seven letters of the alphabet.

TABLATURE graphically represents the guitar fingerboard. Each horizontal line represents a string, and each number represents a fret.

4th string, 2nd fret — 1st & 2nd strings open, played together — open D chord

HALF-STEP BEND: Strike the note and bend up 1/2 step.

WHOLE-STEP BEND: Strike the note and bend up one step.

GRACE NOTE BEND: Strike the note and immediately bend up as indicated.

SLIGHT (MICROTONE) BEND: Strike the note and bend up 1/4 step.

BEND AND RELEASE: Strike the note and bend up as indicated, then release back to the original note. Only the first note is struck.

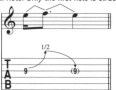

PRE-BEND: Bend the note as indicated, then strike it.

VIBRATO: The string is vibrated by rapidly bending and releasing the note with the fretting hand.

WIDE VIBRATO: The pitch is varied to a greater degree by vibrating with the fretting hand.

HAMMER-ON: Strike the first (lower) note with one finger, then sound the higher note (on the same string) with another finger by fretting it without picking.

PULL-OFF: Place both fingers on the notes to be sounded. Strike the first note and without picking, pull the finger off to sound the second (lower) note.

LEGATO SLIDE: Strike the first note and then slide the same fret-hand finger up or down to the second note. The second note is not struck.

SHIFT SLIDE: Same as legato slide, except the second note is struck.

TRILL: Very rapidly alternate between the notes indicated by continuously hammering on and pulling off.

TAPPING: Hammer ("tap") the fret indicated with the pick-hand index or middle finger and pull off to the note fretted by the fret hand.

NATURAL HARMONIC: Strike the note while the fret-hand lightly touches the string directly over the fret indicated.

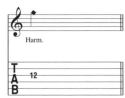

Harm.

PINCH HARMONIC: The note is fretted normally and a harmonic is produced by adding the edge of the thumb or the tip of the index finger of the pick hand to the normal pick attack.

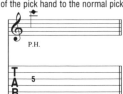

P.H.

PICK SCRAPE: The edge of the pick is rubbed down (or up) the string, producing a scratchy sound.

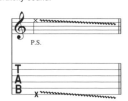

P.S.

MUFFLED STRINGS: A percussive sound is produced by laying the fret hand across the string(s) without depressing, and striking them with the pick hand.

PALM MUTING: The note is partially muted by the pick hand lightly touching the string(s) just before the bridge.

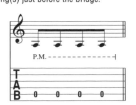

P.M.

RAKE: Drag the pick across the strings indicated with a single motion.

rake

TREMOLO PICKING: The note is picked as rapidly and continuously as possible.

VIBRATO BAR DIVE AND RETURN: The pitch of the note or chord is dropped a specified number of steps (in rhythm), then returned to the original pitch.

w/ bar

VIBRATO BAR SCOOP: Depress the bar just before striking the note, then quickly release the bar.

w/ bar

VIBRATO BAR DIP: Strike the note and then immediately drop a specified number of steps, then release back to the original pitch.

w/ bar